I0133744

I pledge allegiance

To the flag

Of the United States of America

And to the Republic

For which it stands

One Nation

Under God

Indivisible

With liberty and justice

For all

A – All USA Currency Must Always Proclaim "In God We Trust"

B – Balance The Federal Budget

C – Congressional Retirement Benefits Must Be Equal to All Other Federal Employees

D – Duty to God and Country is a Sacred Duty for All of Us

E – Every Law Passed by Congress Must Also Apply to Them and to Their Families

F – Federal Department of Education Should Work Closely with Each State Department of Education

G – Government of the People, By the people, and For the People – Abraham Lincoln

H – Health Care Reform Programs passed by Congress Must Also Apply to Congress

I – I Will Always Pledge Allegiance to the Flag of the United States of America

J – Justice Must Be Applied Equally to All Citizens and to All Elected Government Officials

K – Keep the Goals of Our Founding Fathers Always in Our Mind and in Our Laws

L – Lower our Flag to Half Staff When Needed to Honor Our Fallen Veterans and Patriots

M – Military Strength is Essential to Protect our USA Freedom and Liberty

Your ABC's for Patriotism

26 Ways to Show Our Patriotism in the Land of the Free and the Home of the Brave

James A. Surrell, M.D.
Published by

BEAN BOOKS, LLC, Newberry, Michigan
sosdietdoc@gmail.com

Printing and Layout Stacey Willey
Globe Printing, Inc., Ishpeming, Michigan

ISBN 978-0-9825601-3-6

N – Never, Ever Disrespect, and Especially Never Burn Our American Flag

O – One Nation, Under God, With Liberty and Justice For All

P – Promote and Support the Veterans Administration (VA) to Serve all Our Veterans

Q – Quality Nationwide Local and State Police are Essential to Protect All USA Residents

R – Respect and Follow the Constitution of the United States of America

S – Stand for the National Anthem and Respect the Flag of the USA

T – Thomas Jefferson's Famous Quote in The Declaration of Independence

U – United We Stand, Divided We Fall

V – Value the Contributions of All Our Military Veterans

W – Welcome Others to Become Legal Citizens of Our Great Land of the Free

X – X-out All Disrespect of the Flag of the United States of America

Y – Youth of America Must Be Taught Accurate and Truthful USA History

Z – Zero Tolerance for Anyone Who Disrespects Our Military Veterans

A

**All USA Currency
Must Always Proclaim
"In God We Trust"**

B

Balance The Federal Budget

C

Congressional Retirement Benefits Must Be Equal to All Other Federal Employees

D

**Duty to God and Country
is a Sacred Duty for All of Us**

E

**Every Law Passed by
Congress Must Also
Apply to Them
and to Their Families**

F

Federal Department of Education Should Work Closely with Each State Department of Education

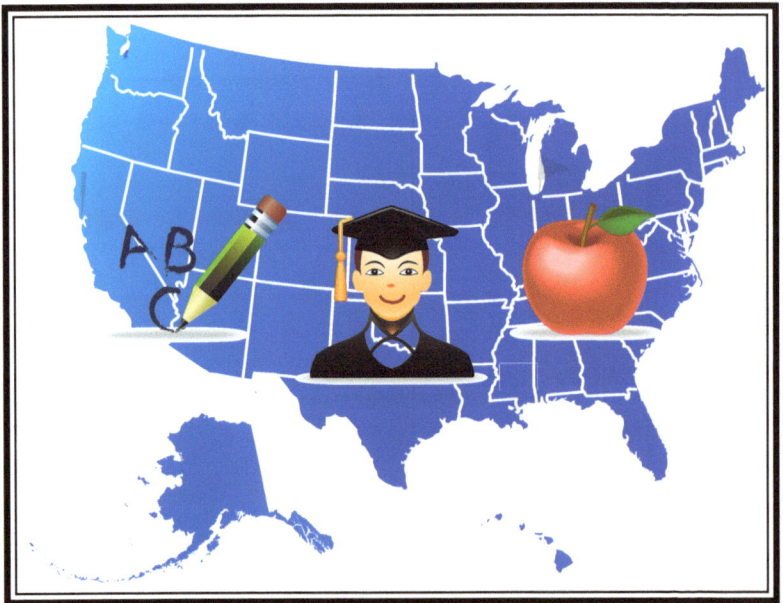

G

**"Government Of the People,
By the people, and
For the People"
– *Abraham Lincoln***

H

Health Care Reform Programs
Passed by Congress
Must Also Apply to Congress

United We Stand

I

I Will Always
Pledge Allegiance to the
Flag of the
United States of America

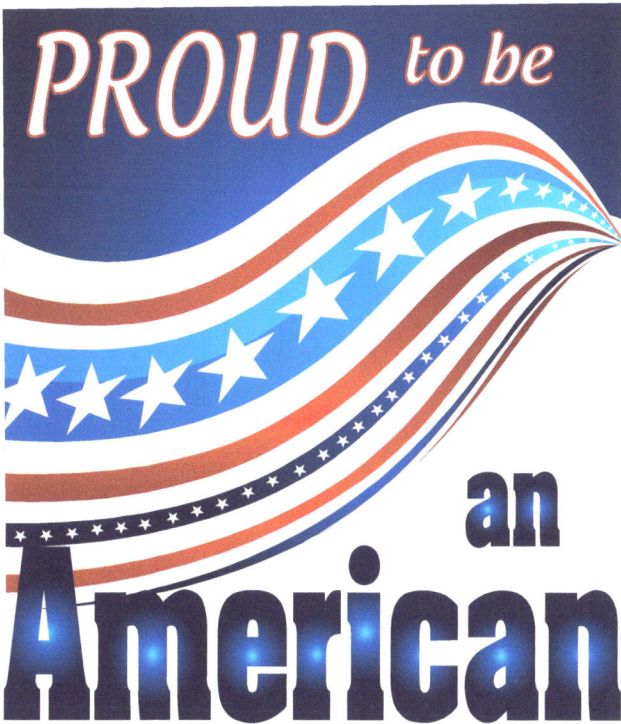

J

**Justice Must Be Applied
Equally to All Citizens
and to All
Elected Government Officials**

K

**Keep the Goals of
Our Founding Fathers
Always in Our Mind
and in Our Laws**

L

Lower Our Flag to Half Staff When Needed to Honor Our Fallen Veterans and Patriots

M

Military Strength is Essential to Protect USA Freedom and Liberty

N

Never, Ever Disrespect, and Especially Never Burn Our American Flag

O

One Nation, Under God, With Liberty and Justice For All

P

Promote and Support the Veterans Administration (VA) to Serve all Our Veterans

Q

Quality Nationwide
Local and State Police are
Essential to Protect
All USA Residents

R

Respect and Follow the Constitution of the United States of America

Constitution of the United States of America

We the People of the United States, in Order to form a more perfect Union, establish Justice, insure domestic Tranquility, provide for the common defense, promote the general Welfare, and secure the Blessings of Liberty to ourselves and our Posterity, do ordain and establish this Constitution for the United States of America.

S

Stand for the National Anthem and Respect the Flag of the USA

American & Proud

T

Thomas Jefferson's Famous Quote in The Declaration of Independence

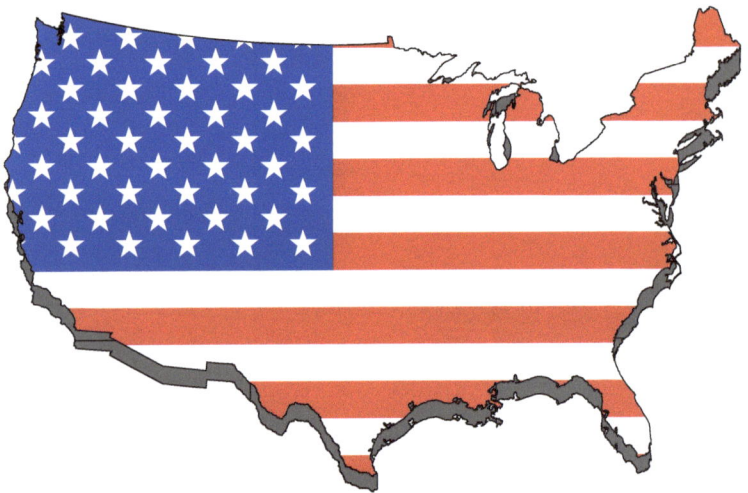

"We hold these truths to be self-evident, that all men are created equal, that they are endowed by their Creator with certain unalienable rights, that among these are Life, Liberty, and the Pursuit of Happiness."

U

United We Stand,
Divided We Fall

V

**Value the Contributions of
All Our Military Veterans**

Thank You

VETERANS

REMEMBER AND HONOR

★ ★ ★

W

**Welcome Others to Become
Legal Citizens
of Our Great Land of the Free**

PROUD TO

BECOME AN
AMERICAN

X

X-out Any Disrespect
of the Flag of the
United States of America

Y

Youth of America
Must Be Taught
Accurate and Truthful
USA History

Z

**Zero Tolerance for Anyone
Who Disrespects
Our Military Veterans**

Land of the Free

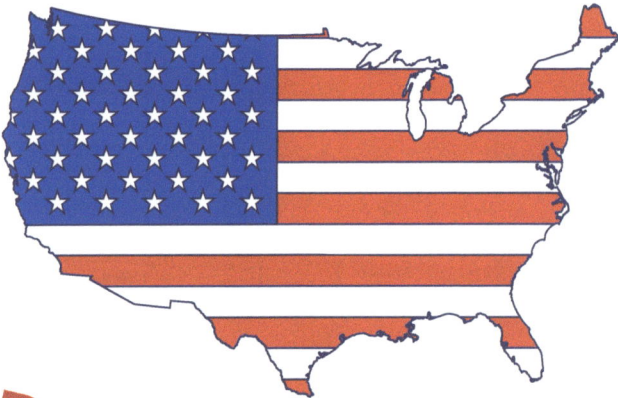

Because of the Brave